DUKE ELLINGTON

CONTENTS

Arranged by Dan Towey

Cover photography: Frank Driggs Collection
Used by permission

ISBN 0-634-00653-3

HAL•LEONARD®
CORPORATION
7777 W. BLUEMOUND RD. P.O. BOX 13819 MILWAUKEE, WI 53213

Visit Hal Leonard Online at
www.halleonard.com

DUKE ELLINGTON

Duke Ellington titled his biography *Music Is My Mistress* and, along with his song "It Don't Mean a Thing (If It Ain't Got That Swing"), it succinctly sums up the man and his philosophy. With the centennial of his birth in 1999, the spotlight is once again shining on his remarkable achievements. He created over 1500 compositions along with countless arrangements, and led one of the most influential and *swinging* orchestras of the 20th century, through which passed some of the greatest jazz instrumentalists of all time. A refined and elegant man of broad artistic tastes, he set a standard of excellence in his 50-year career that may never be equaled.

Edward Kennedy "Duke" Ellington was born in Washington, D.C. on April 29, 1899. Unlike many of his contemporaries from the South, he grew up in a middle-class society family that provided him with the confidence and self-esteem to carry himself with dignity his entire life. Despite a consuming interest in baseball (that proved to be a distraction), Ellington began piano lessons at the age of seven, and even though he had developed a keen interest in ragtime and barrelhouse piano, did not take the instrument seriously until several years later. After hearing a talented pianist in Philadelphia on the way back from summer vacation in Asbury Park, New Jersey, he finally sat down with a purpose and composed his first piece, "Soda Fountain Rag." By this time he had acquired his nickname from an upwardly mobile high school friend who decided Ellington should have a classy "title" if he was going to travel in high society. In 1917 he started playing professionally in Washington and relocated to New York in 1923 as bandleader of the Washingtonians, eventually displaying the influences of Willie "The Lion" Smith, James P. Johnson, and Fats Waller in his piano style.

Ellington made his recording debut in 1924 and went on to issue titles through 1926 to little fanfare. However, later in that year, the band released their first theme song, "East St. Louis Toddle-oo" (later covered by Steely Dan) and "Birmingham Breakdown." Along with "Black and Tan Fantasy," "Creole Love Call," and a gig at the Cotton Club that followed in 1927, the Duke Ellington Orchestra had arrived. Except for a brief period during the early fifties when virtually all big bands struggled, his glorious career continued unabated, literally up until his death on May 24, 1974. Despite the expected turnover in personnel, he survived the changing musical trends of every era, including bebop, which he liked and smoothly incorporated into his sound. In addition to an unparalleled catalog of jazz standards, Ellington also left as his legacy a number of ambitious suites, sacred music which he composed in the sixties, appearances in films, and movie soundtracks.

The guitar was never a featured solo voice in the Duke Ellington Orchestra (like most bands of the swing era), although the legendary Lonnie Johnson guested on a number of sides in 1928 to Duke's appreciation. Part of this was due to the lack of amplification before the late thirties and the reluctance of many bandleaders to see the guitar beyond its traditional role as a time-keeping rhythm instrument. Fred Guy joined the band full-time as a banjoist shortly after they relocated to New York, then switching to guitar in 1933. Teddy Bunn took his place for eighteen months in the late twenties, and recorded with Ellington in 1929. Guy played strictly rhythm, as did Freddie Green in Count Basie's band, until his departure in 1947. Ellington never replaced him, although he once expressed admiration for Kenny Burrell. Nonetheless, due to the strong blues and swing influences that show up in the melodies and riffs, Ellington's music lends itself to guitar interpretation.

The fifteen classics that follow are arrangements based on the orchestral recordings, not transcriptions of guitar parts. The resulting music is extremely melodic with cool, single-note lines and hip chord voicings that blend seamlessly. They are a fitting tribute to the immortal music and genius of Duke Ellington.

–Dave Rubin

Caravan
from SOPHISTICATED LADIES

Words and Music by Duke Ellington, Irving Mills and Juan Tizol

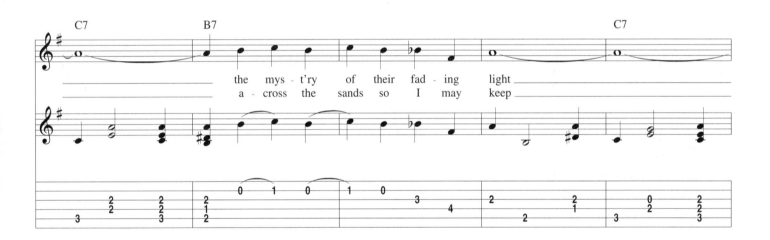

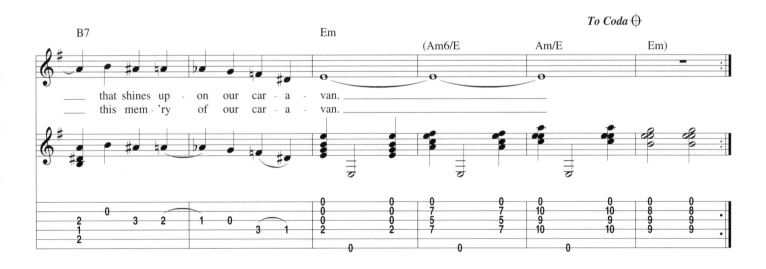

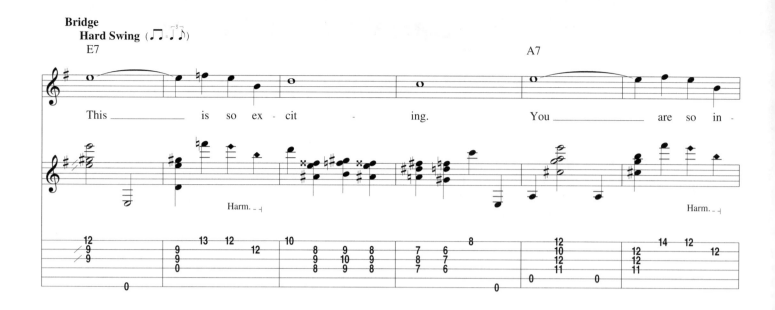

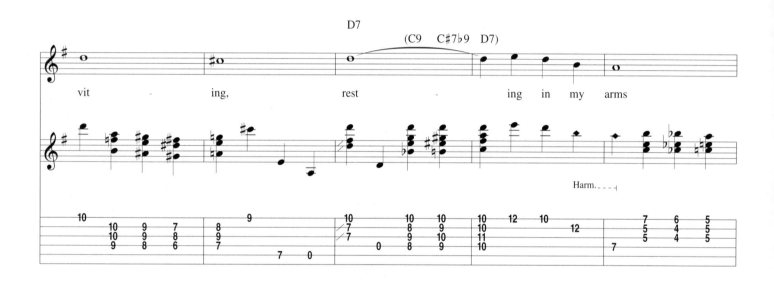

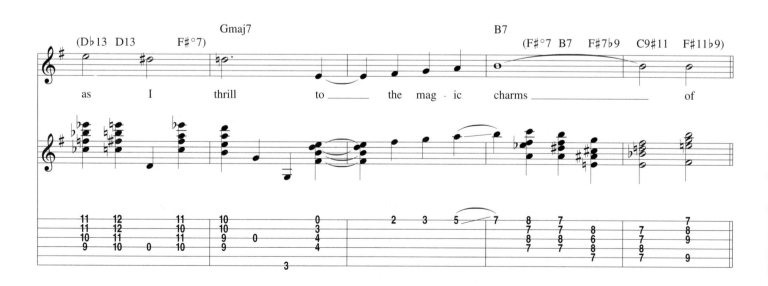

D.C. al Coda

⊕ *Coda*

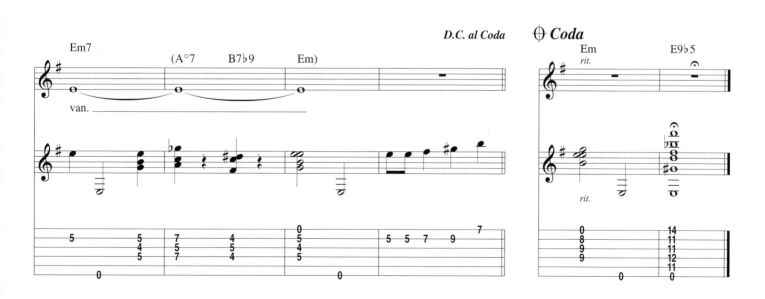

Come Sunday
from BLACK, BROWN & BEIGE

By Duke Ellington

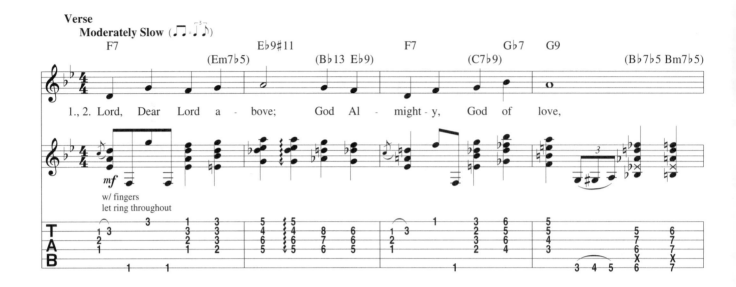

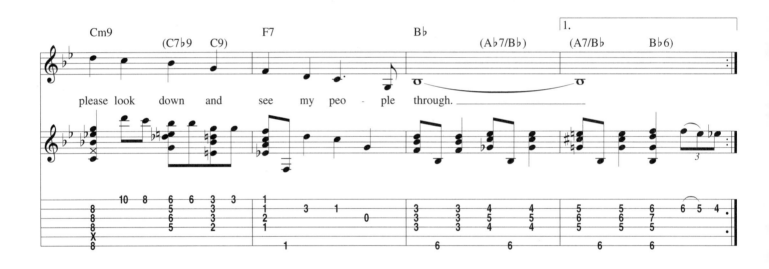

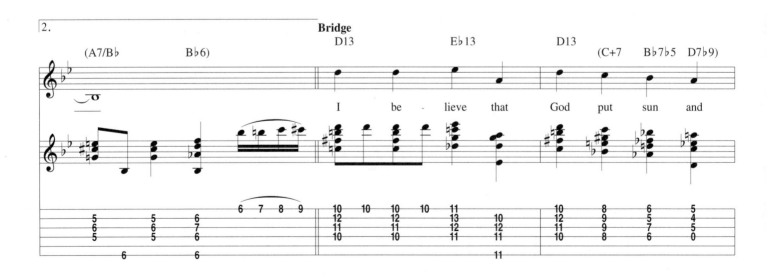

Do Nothin' Till You Hear From Me

Words and Music by Bob Russell and Duke Ellington

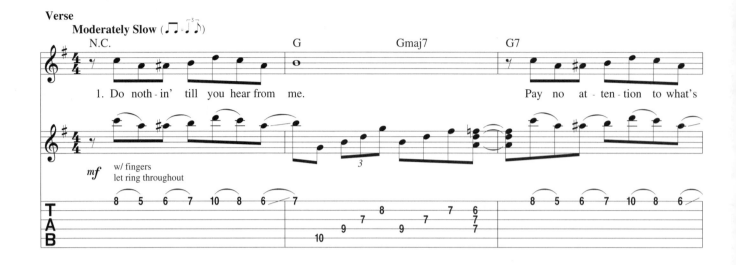

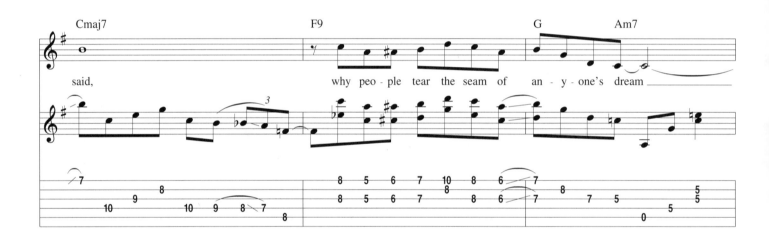

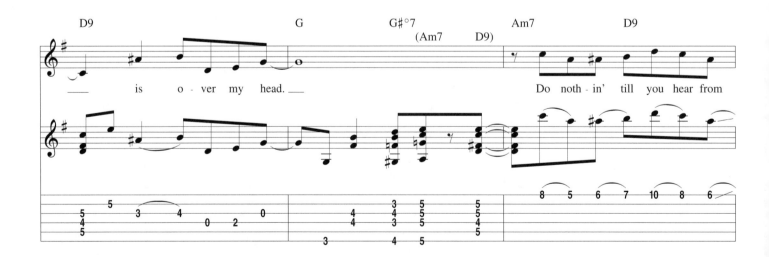

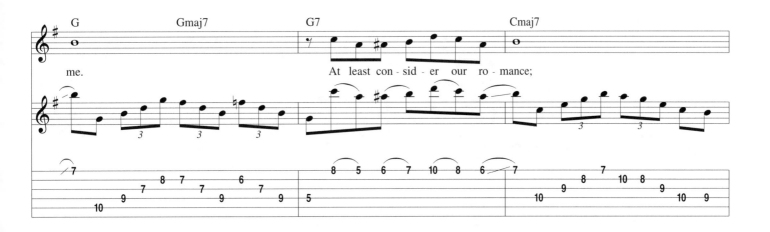

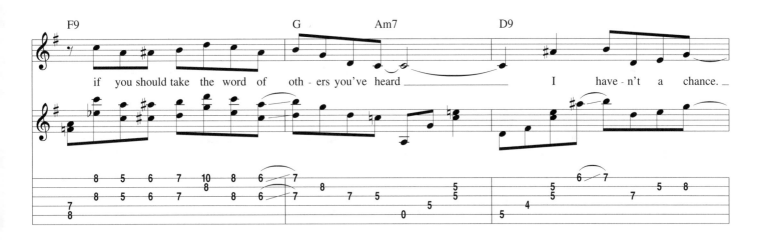

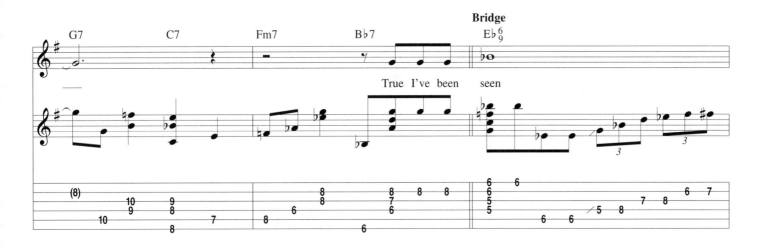

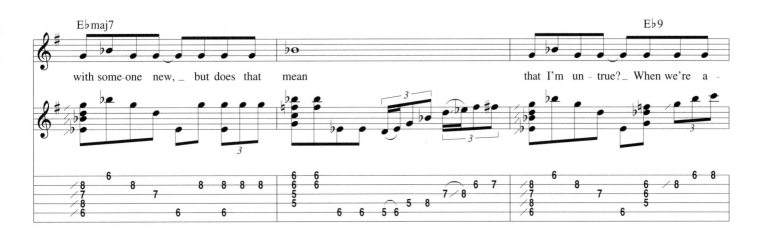

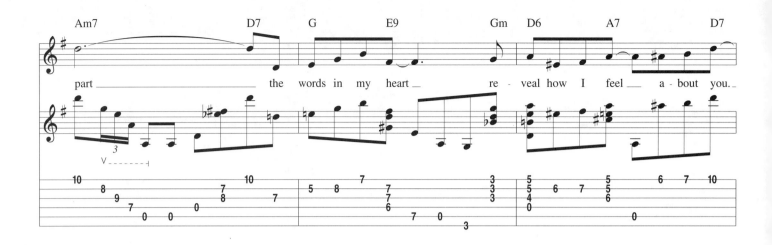

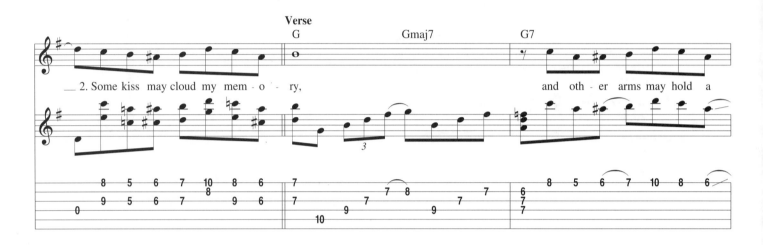

*T = Thumb on ⑥

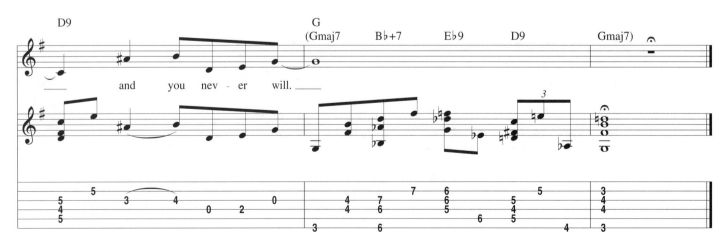

Don't Get Around Much Anymore

Words and Music by Bob Russell and Duke Ellington

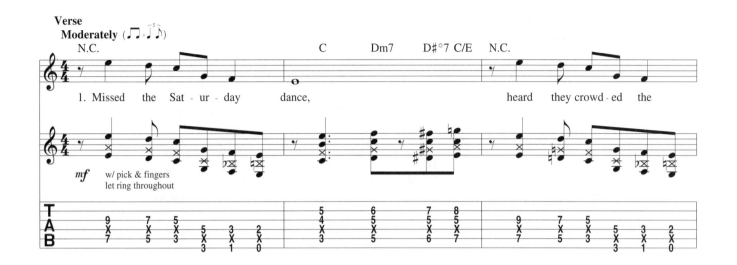

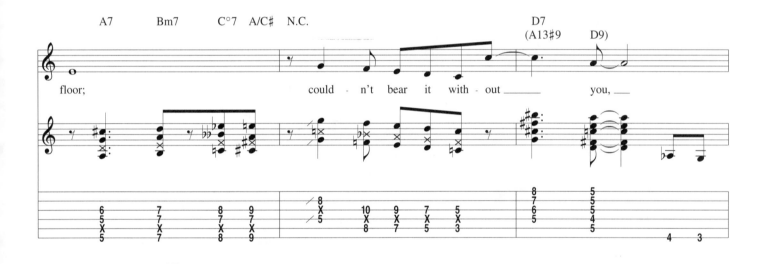

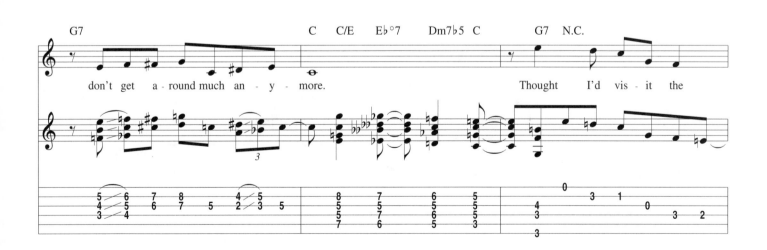

I Got It Bad and That Ain't Good

Words by Paul Francis Webster
Music by Duke Ellington

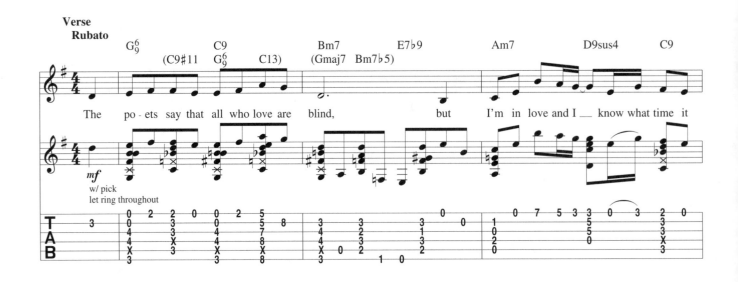

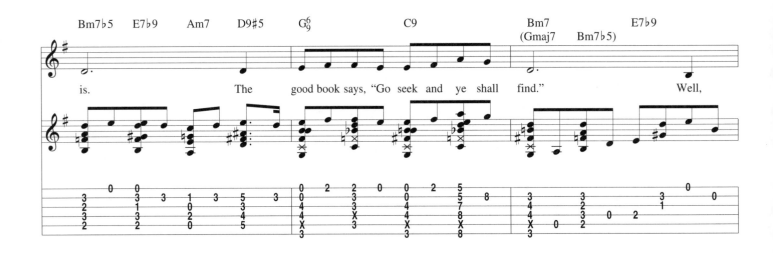

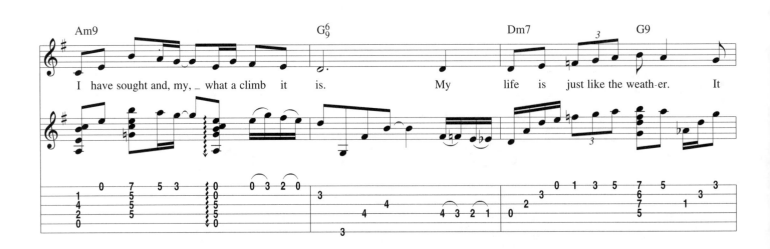

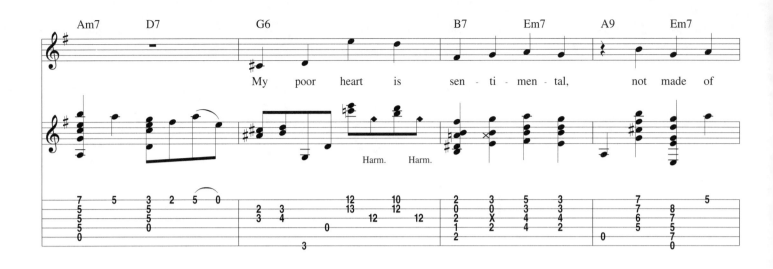

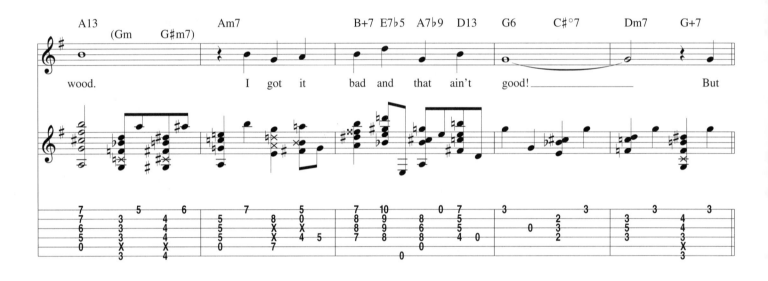

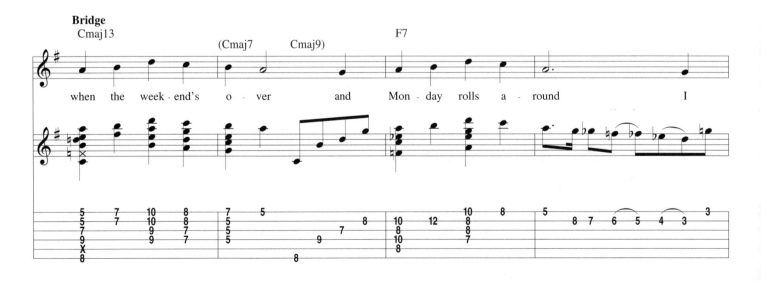

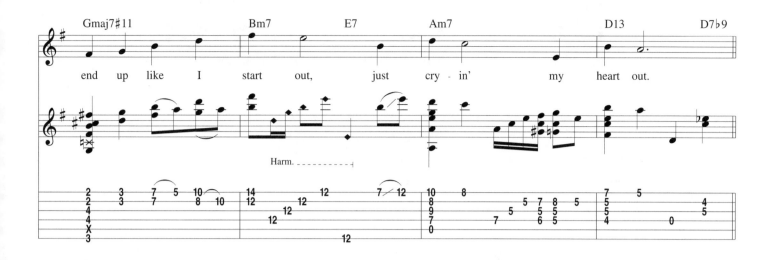

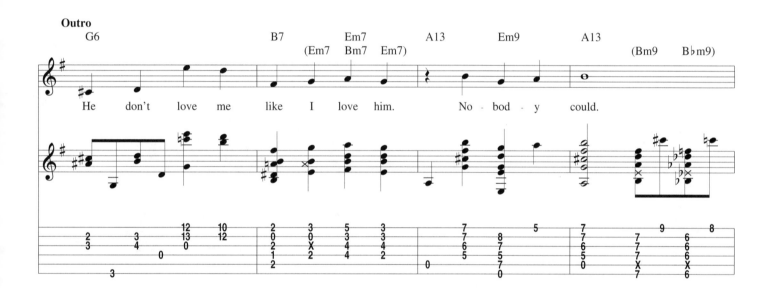

I Let a Song Go Out of My Heart

Words and Music by Duke Ellington, Henry Nemo, John Redmond and Irving Mills

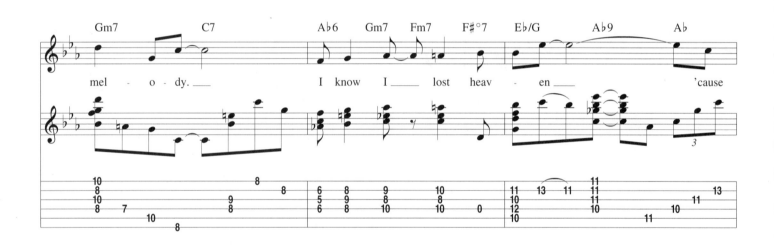

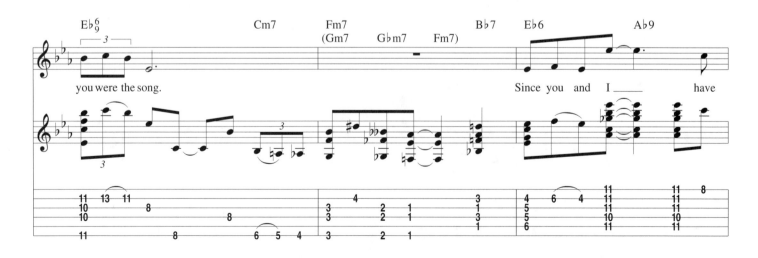

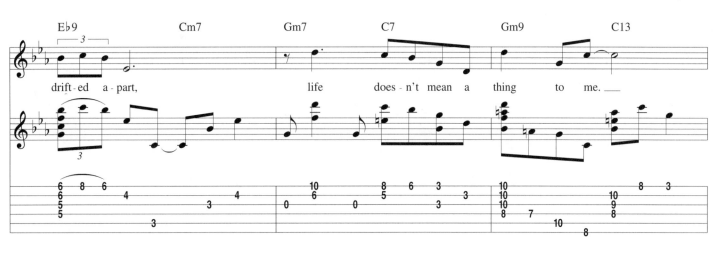

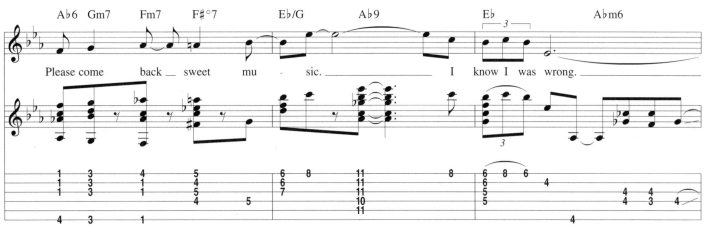

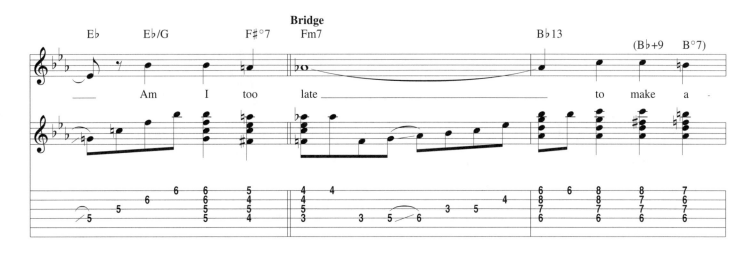

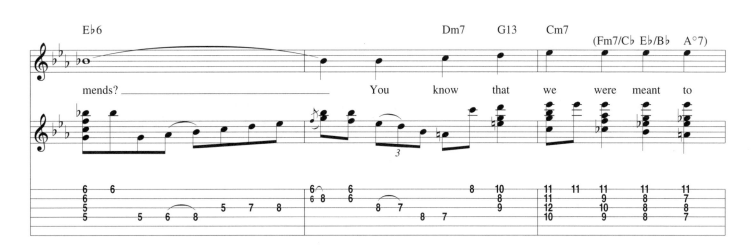

I'm Just a Lucky So and So

Words by Mack David
Music by Duke Ellington

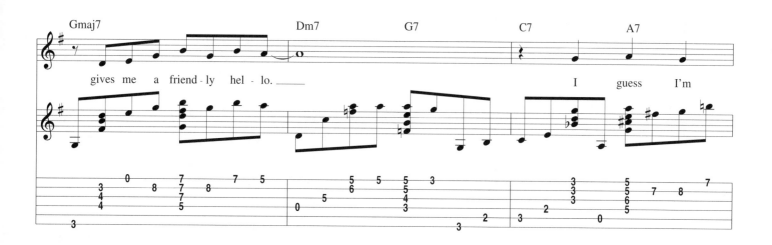

Verse

3. And when the day is through _ each night I hur - ry to ___

a home where love waits, I know. _ I guess I'm

just a luck - y so - and - so. ___

In a Sentimental Mood

Words and Music by Duke Ellington, Irving Mills and Manny Kurtz

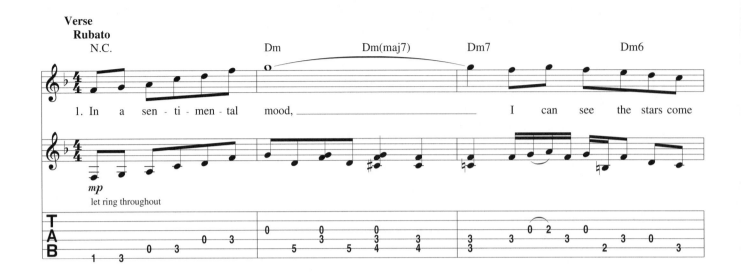

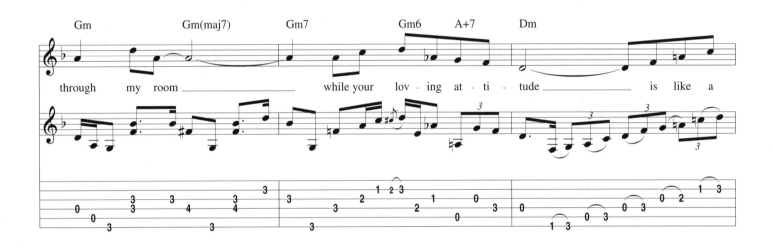

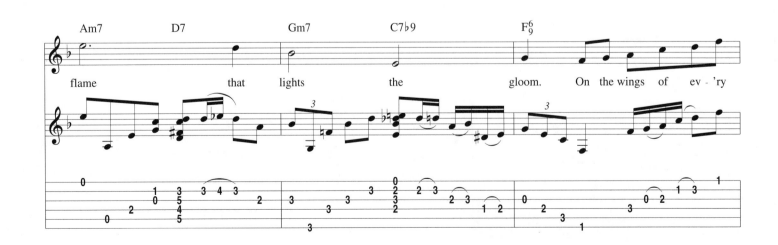

It Don't Mean a Thing
(If It Ain't Got That Swing)
from SOPHISTICATED LADIES

Words and Music by Duke Ellington and Irving Mills

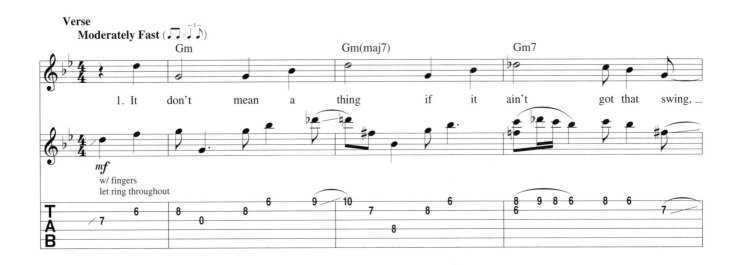

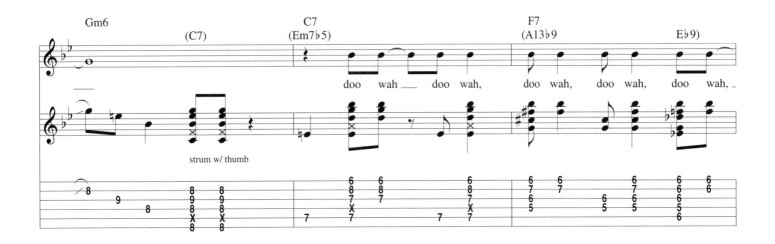

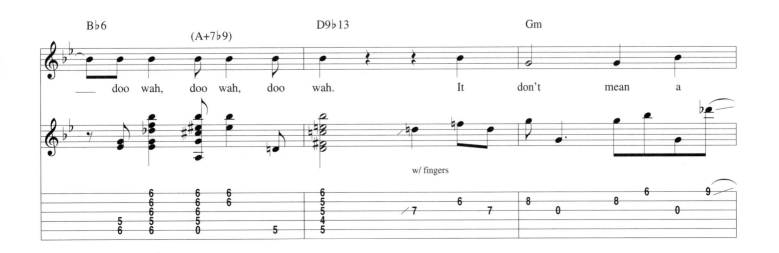

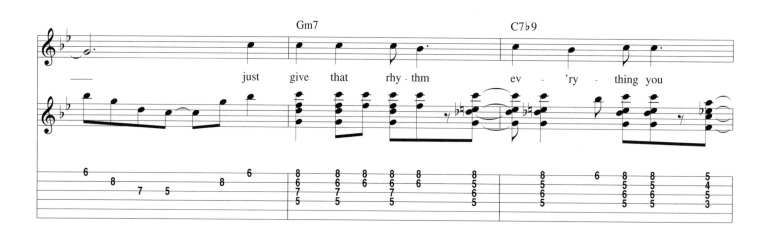

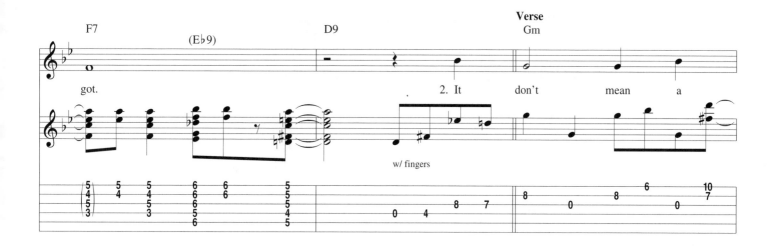

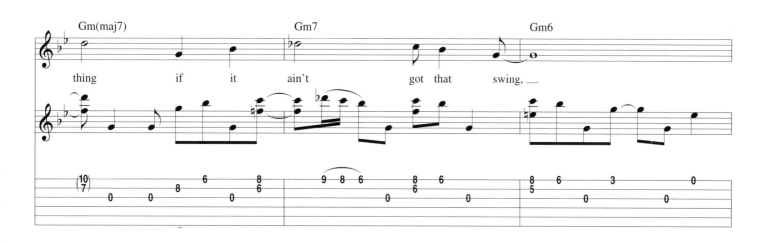

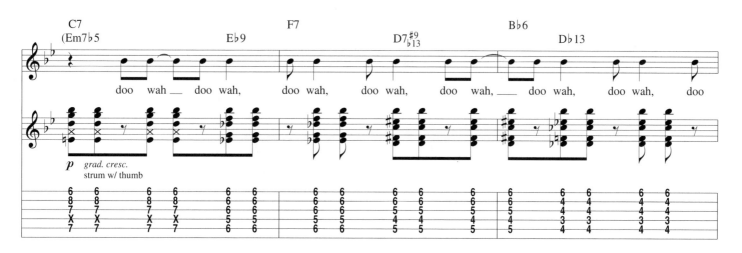

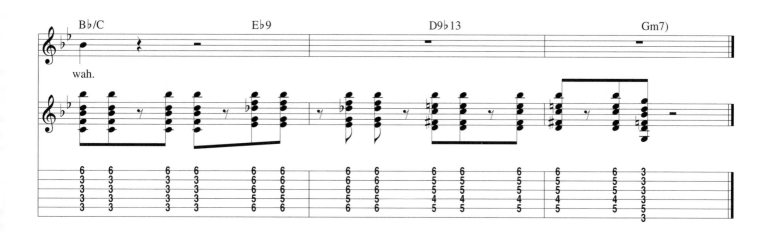

Mood Indigo
from SOPHISTICATED LADIES

Words and Music by Duke Ellington, Irving Mills and Albany Bigard

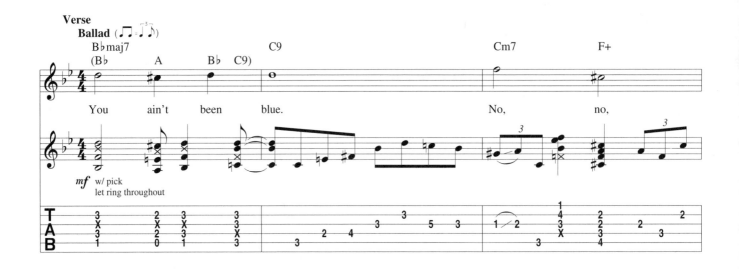

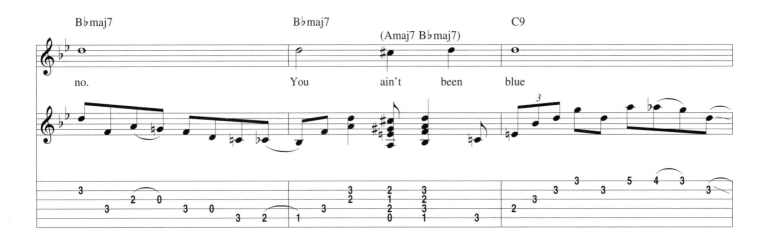

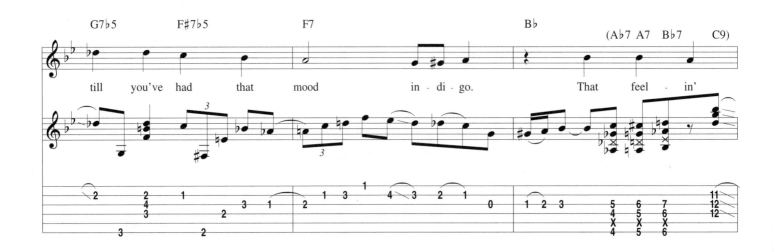

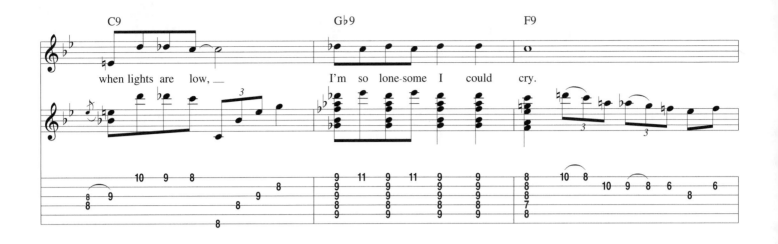

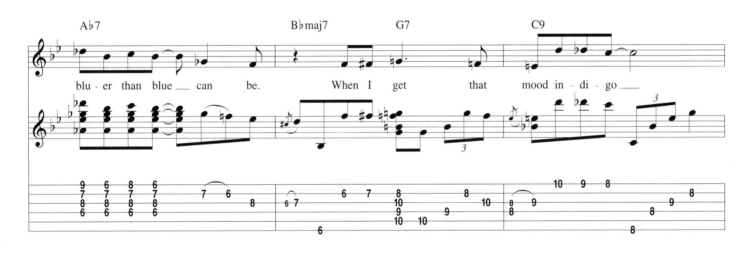

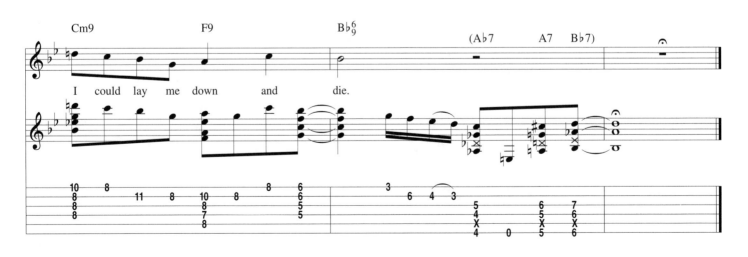

Prelude to a Kiss

Words by Irving Gordon and Irving Mills
Music by Duke Ellington

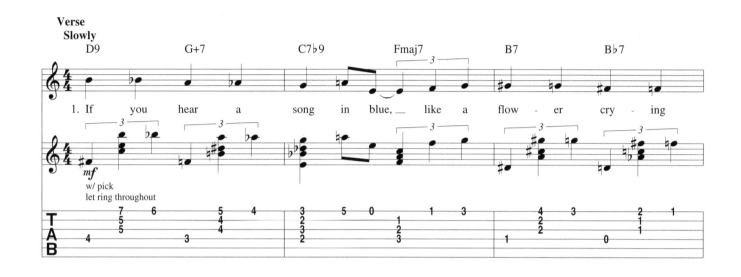

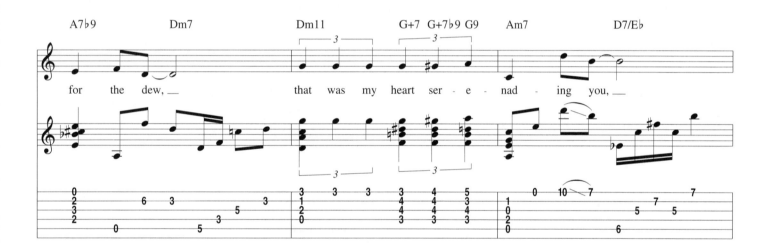

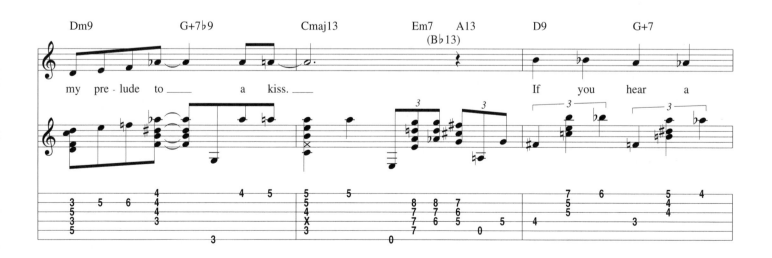

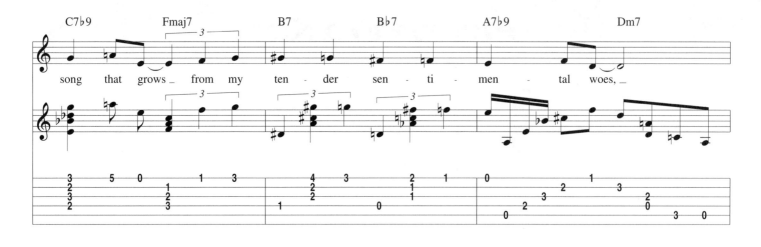

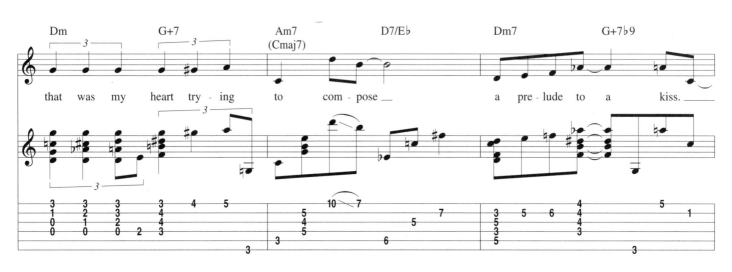

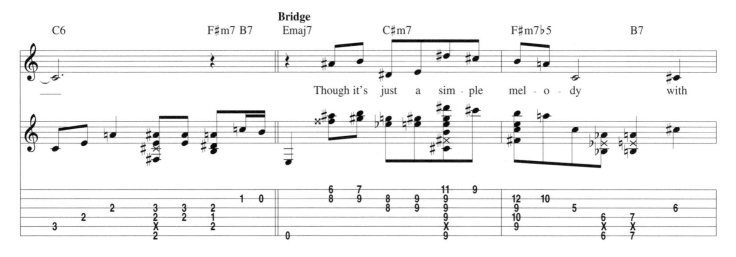

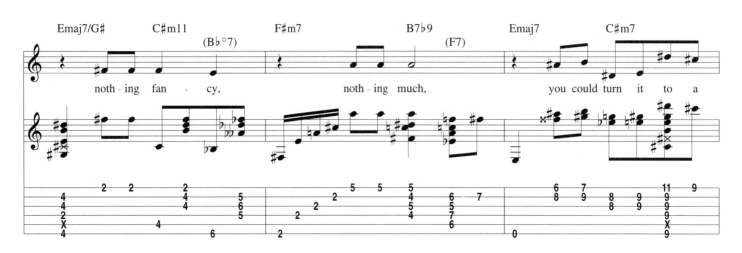

Satin Doll

from SOPHISTICATED LADIES

Words by Johnny Mercer and Billy Strayhorn
Music by Duke Ellington

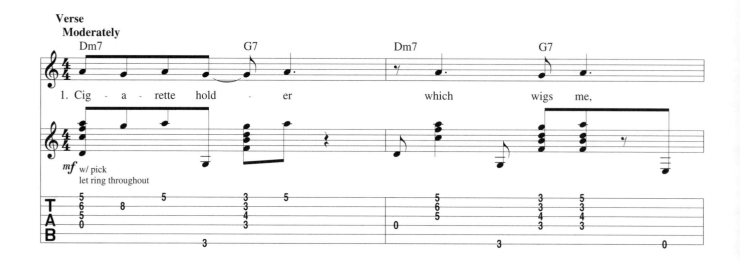

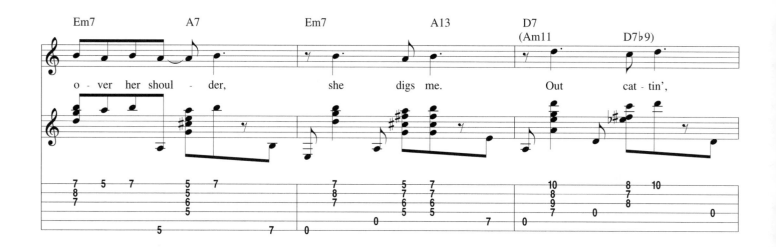

give it a whirl __ but I ain't for no girl catch-in' me, __

Verse

switch - e - roo - ney. 3. Tel - e - phone num - bers, well, you know.

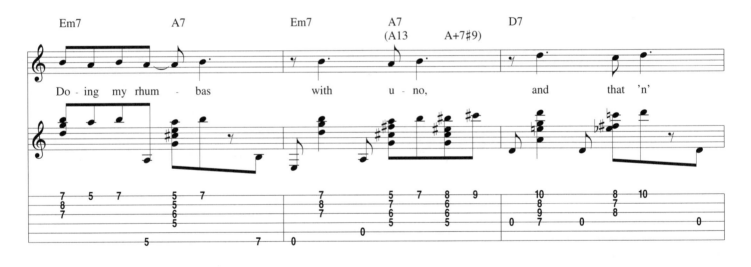

Do - ing my rhum - bas with u - no, and that 'n'

my sat - in doll. __

Solitude

Words and Music by Duke Ellington, Eddie De Lange and Irving Mills

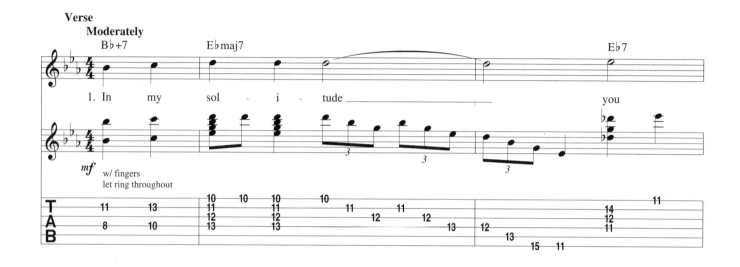

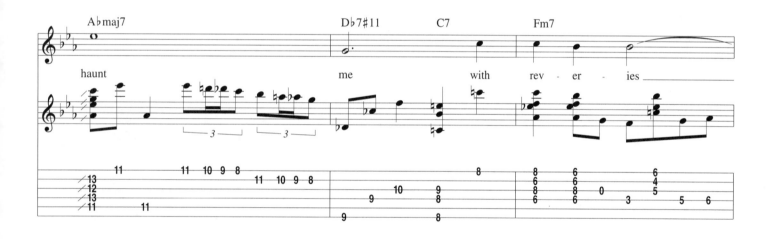

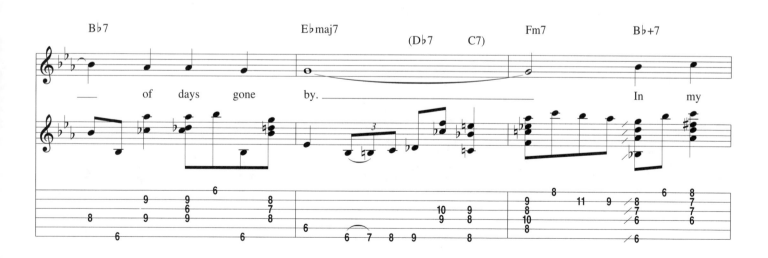

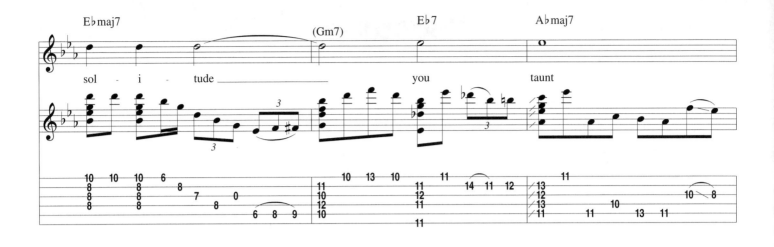

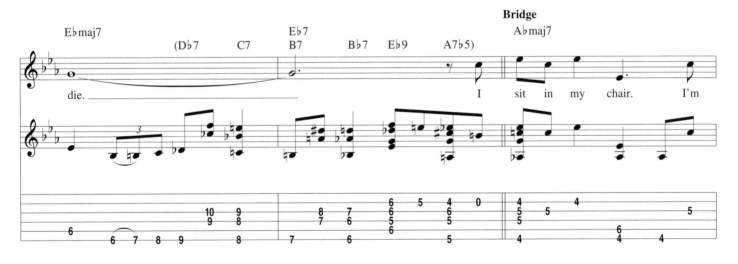

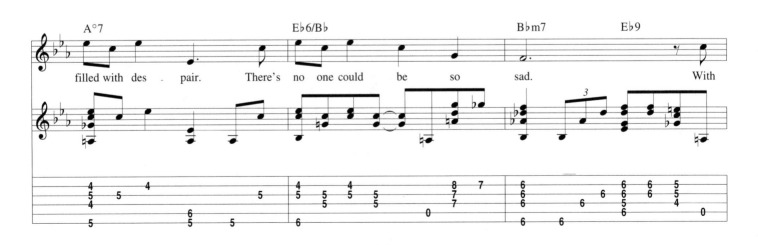

Sophisticated Lady

from SOPHISTICATED LADIES

Words and Music by Duke Ellington, Irving Mills and Mitchell Parish

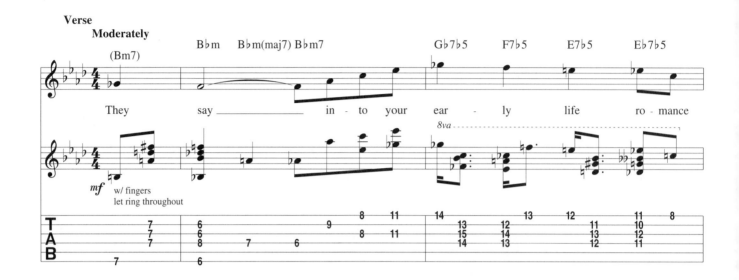

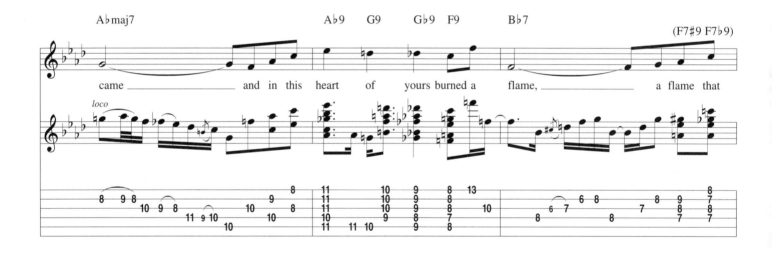

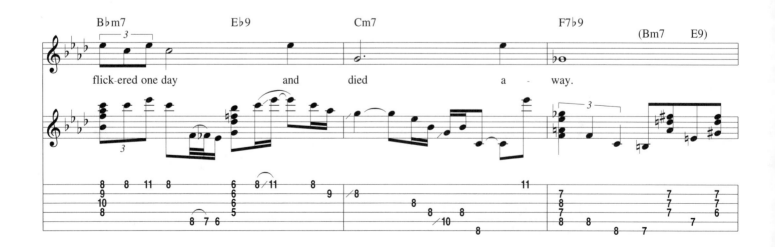

Take the "A" Train

Words and Music by Billy Strayhorn

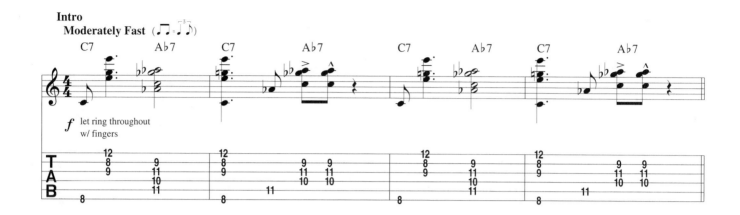

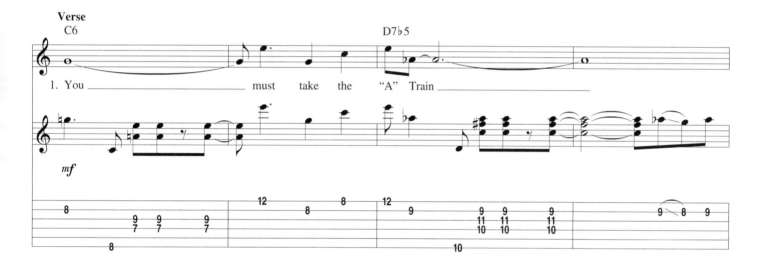

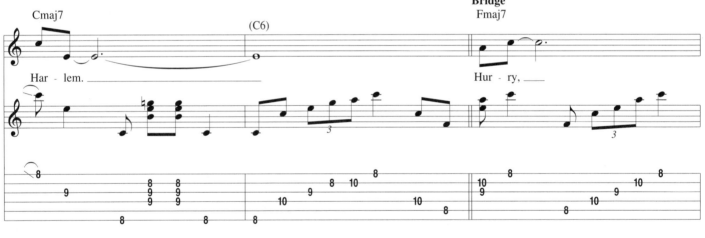

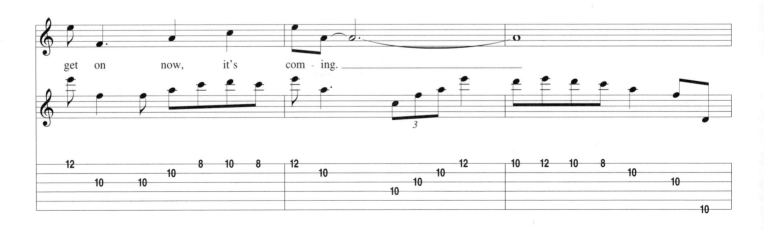

PLAY LIKE THE PROS

Jazz Instruction & Transcriptions from Hal Leonard

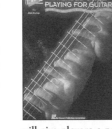

Prices, contents and availability subject to change without notice.